(A SET OF 5 BOOKS)

3

GRANDPA'S STORIES

(STORIES FOR CHILDREN)

To entertain children is to worship God.
— *Sane Guruji*

Editor of the stories retold
Mohanbhai S. Patel M.A.

Illustrations
Prakash Bandekar

Adaptation
Asmita Bhatt

: STORIES :

1. THE SUPPORT

2. POISONOUS SWEETS

3. A TRUE DISCIPLE

4. A LESSON

5. BORROWED GRANDEUR

6. NATURE'S CREATION

7. BALU SHEDS HIS FEAR

navNeet ®

Price : ₹ 45.00 (BOOK 3)

F 4523

1. THE SUPPORT

It was autumn. All the trees started shedding their leaves. The leaves of the old *peepul* tree turned yellow. Soon the *peepul* tree would shed its dry leaves.

One day, there was a strong wind and a *peepul* leaf fell off the branch of the tree. It landed on a lump of earth. The leaf requested the lump, "Will you please give me some support? Otherwise, I will be blown far away by this strong wind."

The lump of earth was arrogant and short-tempered. It bluntly said, "Sorry. I will not give you any support." Meanwhile, a strong wind blew and the leaf was blown away with the wind.

It started drizzling. Now the lump of earth was frightened. Suddenly, another *peepul* leaf fell on it. The lump pleaded, "Dear leaf, please cover me; otherwise I will melt in this rain."

The leaf replied, "Just a few minutes ago, you refused to give any support to a leaf. Now why should I help you?"

The sky was covered with dark clouds. It started raining heavily and there was thunder and lightning. The leaf pitied the lump of earth. It said to the lump, "I am not selfish and heartless like you. I will cover you."

Saying this, the leaf called two other leaves and together, they covered the lump to protect it. After it had stopped raining, the lump was still dry and intact.

The leaf said, "I hope you have learnt a lesson today. You should know that we all survive with one another's support. In fact, the whole world survives on mutual support."

SUPPORT HELPS SURVIVAL

2. POISONOUS SWEETS

Mulla Nasiruddin visited the village school once a week. He taught the students religion and morality. One day, on his way to school, he bought a box of sweets.

Mulla Nasiruddin reached the school and began teaching the students. It so happened that the Mulla had to go out for some important work at that time. So he put the box of sweets on a high shelf in his room. He said to the students sitting in the room, "Now listen to me carefully. There is poison in the sweets in this box. So please do not eat the sweets."

Saying this, the Mulla left the room.

Mulla Nasiruddin's nephew was also present in that room. He said to his friends, "Let's eat the sweets. There is no poison in it. My uncle doesn't want us to eat the sweets, and so he has tried to frighten us by saying that there is poison in it."

All the students agreed with the Mulla's nephew. One of the tall and strong boys stood under the shelf. Another boy climbed on his shoulders. They reached the shelf and took the box of sweets. In a few minutes, the box was empty.

After eating the sweets, the Mulla's nephew picked up the Mulla's knife lying on the table and broke it.

After some time, Mulla Nasiruddin returned to his room. He saw the broken knife and was angry. Suddenly, he looked up at the shelf and found the box of sweets missing. Furious, the Mulla screamed, "Who has eaten these sweets?"

All the students pointed at his nephew.

Mulla Nasiruddin's nephew started sobbing loudly and said in a broken voice, "I wanted to sharpen the broken point of my pencil. So, I took your knife. As I was sharpening the pencil, the knife fell down and the blade broke. I was sure that you would be angry with me and would break my bones for this offence. I was so scared that I decided to commit suicide by eating the poisonous sweets. I ate some, but there was no effect of the poison. So, at last, I ate all the sweets in the box. But I am surprised that I am still alive!"

Hearing his nephew's explanation, Mulla Nasiruddin burst into laughter. He said, "My dear nephew! You are a match for your uncle. Till today, I was under the impression that there was no one as clever and witty as I. But I am pleased with your ready wit. I pardon you for your offence!"

3. A TRUE DISCIPLE

Samarth Ramdas was the *Guru* of Chhatrapati Shivaji Maharaj. Ramdas had many disciples. Ambadas was one of them. He would gladly do all that his teacher asked him to do. He was always very eager to serve his teacher.

The other disciples considered Ambadas to be a fool and they made fun of him. But Ambadas was not bothered. He was engrossed in the service of his teacher.

One day, Ramdas was going out somewhere with his disciples. On their way, they came across a well. There was a huge neem tree near the well. One of the branches of the tree hung exactly over the well. Ramdas and his disciples decided to take some rest; so they sat down under the neem tree.

After some time, Ramdas said to his disciples, "Who will chop off that branch hanging over the well?" Ramdas looked at one of the disciples. Giving him a saw, he said, "Climb the tree and chop the branch off from the trunk with this saw."

The disciple said, "But *Guruji*, I do not know how to climb a tree."

Ramdas then asked another disciple to chop off the branch. The disciple said, "I do not know how to use a saw. But I can chop off the branch with an axe."

Ramdas asked yet another disciple to do the job. The disciple said, "If I chop the branch off from the trunk, I will fall into the well."

Thus, not a single disciple was ready to cut the branch of the neem tree. They were afraid that they might get hurt or might lose their lives. At last, Ramdas called Ambadas and said, "Will you chop off the branch?"

Without a moment's hesitation, Ambadas took the saw and climbed the tree. As asked by Ramdas, he began to chop the branch off from the trunk. All the other disciples laughed at his folly. But Ambadas ignored them and continued to chop off the branch. As soon as the branch was chopped off from the trunk of the tree, it fell into the well along with Ambadas. Now the disciples were frightened. But Ramdas was unperturbed. He said, "There is no need to worry about Ambadas. He is safe and sound. He has faith in me and no harm will come to him."

After some time, Ambadas climbed out of the well. He bowed to Ramdas and said, "*Guruji*, do not worry. I am safe. I am not hurt."

Ramdas told his disciples, "Do you see this young ·man? All of you think that he is a fool and you make fun of him. But he has so much faith in the words of his teacher."

The disciples were ashamed of themselves and realized their mistake.

4. A LESSON

There was a temple in a small village. The priest of the temple was a learned man. He was revered as a saint.

There also lived, in this village, a girl named Lalita. She was very fond of gossiping. She gossiped about her family, her relatives and neighbours. Her idle talk worried her parents. One day, they approached the priest of the temple to seek his advice. The priest agreed to help them. The following day, he called Lalita to the temple.

Giving her a pot filled with jujubes, he said, "My dear girl, take this pot. I want you to go home and return to the temple immediately. But you must drop each and every jujube on your way home and back here."

Lalita followed the priest's instructions. On her way home and back to the temple, she dropped all the jujubes from the pot.

When Lalita returned to the temple, the priest patted her and praised her. Then he said, "Now go home with this empty pot and return to the temple again. But on your way home and back here, collect all the jujubes which you had dropped and scattered earlier."

Lalita argued, "*Maharaj*, I am prepared to do as you say. But a few jujubes might have been trampled under the feet of people and buried under the soil. The sparrows also might have eaten some. How can I collect all the jujubes?"

The priest said, "You are right, my girl! You know that you cannot collect all the scattered jujubes; similarly, you must understand that words once spoken cannot be taken back. Therefore, one should not speak without thinking. One must control one's tongue."

Lalita understood what the priest wanted to convey to her. She realized her mistake. She resolved that she would never utter a word without thinking. She thanked the priest and went home. Lalita then led a very happy life.

5. BORROWED GRANDEUR

It was evening. The sun was about to set in the horizon. White clouds filled the blue sky in the west.

The golden rays of the setting sun filled the clouds with a variety of colours.

Down on the earth, the wheat fields swayed in the cool evening breeze. Colourful butterflies fluttered over the crops. Suddenly, one of them looked up towards the sky and saw the colourful clouds floating above and said, "Ah! Look up there. Beautiful fairies are dancing in the sky!"

The clouds floating in the sky looked down on the earth. They saw the butterflies and found their lovely and colourful wings inferior to their own beauty.

The proud clouds considered the butterflies inferior to them.

But the butterflies had their own colours.

The clouds had borrowed their colours from the rays of the setting sun. How long would those colours last?

The sun was setting gradually. Its light also became dimmer. The colours of the clouds were also fading with the setting sun. The butterflies looked at the fading colours of the clouds. However, their own colours were the same as before! After all, they had colours of their own. But the clouds owed their colours to the sun.

The clouds looked beautiful because of their borrowed colours and yet they were proud of their beauty. But what would happen to them when the sun had set?

Soon the sun set. It grew dark. The clouds, too, became dark. Their borrowed colours had faded. They now realized that their beauty was momentary, because it was borrowed. They were ashamed of their false pride. The butterflies still looked as beautiful as ever in their own colours.

6. NATURE'S CREATION

One evening, King Bhoja and Kalidas, the poet, were taking a stroll on the bank of a river. The farmers had sown seeds of watermelons and muskmelons in the bed of the river. Creepers had grown along the ground and there were big, ripe watermelons and muskmelons on them. There were many banyan trees, too, on the banks of the river. These trees were laden with tiny, red fruits.

King Bhoja looked at the fruits and said, "Kalidas, I wonder why there are such big fruits on those delicate creepers and such tiny fruits on these big banyan trees! What could be the reason behind such disproportionate creations of Nature?"

"Your Majesty, there is always a sensible reason behind every creation of Nature," said Kalidas.

"But I see no sense in these creations. Look at the huge banyan tree and look at its tiny fruits! What could be the reason for this?" argued the King, who was not satisfied with Kalidas' answer.

Continuing their discussion, King Bhoja and Kalidas went further. They saw a man resting under a banyan tree. There were ripe, red fruits on it. Suddenly, there was a strong gust of wind. One of the fruits of the banyan tree fell on the head of the man who was resting under the tree! The man woke up with a scream. King Bhoja and Kalidas noticed this.

Kalidas said, "Your Majesty! Did you see that? Can you imagine what would have happened if a big fruit like a watermelon or a muskmelon had fallen on that man's head? That was why I said that there is a sensible reason behind Nature's creation of big watermelons and tiny fruits of the banyan tree."

King Bhoja thought for a while and said, "I agree with you. I now understand that there is a sensible reason behind every creation of Nature."

7. BALU SHEDS HIS FEAR

Balu was his grandmother's pet. He was born after many years of his parents' marriage. So he was pampered by everybody.

Though Balu was now no longer a toddler, his parents and grandmother took a lot of care and never left him alone. As soon as he stepped out of the door, grandmother would say, "Balu dear! Be careful. That dog may bite you." Balu wished to play with the calf tied in the cowshed. But his father would say, "Son! Do not go there. The cow may butt you with her horns."

Grandmother would not allow Balu to go out on a windy day. Balu loved to play in the rain. But when the sky was covered with dark clouds and there was thunder and lightning, his father would say, "Balu, do not be afraid, my son! I am here with you." Thus, Balu grew up to be a nervous and timid boy. He was always dependent on others for everything.

Balu's mother was always worried, "I wish Balu were fearless."

One day, Balu's grandmother fell ill. Even after two days, the temperature would not go down. There was no doctor in the village. Who would go and call the doctor from the nearby town? Balu's father said, "Now Balu is a big boy. He can very well go to the town to fetch the doctor." Balu's mother hesitantly agreed. She said, "Yes. He is a big boy, but he is so chicken-hearted!"

However, Balu's father called him and said, "Balu, your grandmother has been ill for the last two days. Her temperature is not going down. Go to the town immediately and fetch Dr Mukund here, will you?"

Balu took his bicycle and rode to the town. It soon began to grow dark. There were huge, shady trees on either side of the road. Balu saw strange shapes of the trees in the dark.

Now Balu was scared. He trembled with fear. He did not have the courage to utter even a single word! How then could he shout for help? There was a big banyan tree along the road. When Balu looked at it, he saw a figure. He thought that it was ghost jumping down from the tree!

At home, Balu's parents were waiting for him to return with the doctor. Hours passed, but there was no sign of Balu and the doctor. Balu's mother was worried and she said to her husband, "Listen. I am here to take care of mother. Will you please go and search for Balu? Go and find out what has happened to him. Why is he delayed? I am worried because he is such a chicken-hearted fellow!"

Balu's father took a torch and a stick with him and went in search of Balu. As he was walking hurriedly on the road to the town, he suddenly saw someone standing near the banyan tree. He stopped there and shouted, "Balu! Balu! Is that you?"

Balu was relieved to hear his father's voice. He ran to him and put his arms around him. He said in a broken voice, "Papa! Oh! I am so happy to see you here. But look! Look, there is a ghost there!"

Balu's father flashed his torch in the direction of the banyan tree. And what did he see? There were two big monkeys there! They were jumping up and down the banyan tree.

Balu's father said, "Look carefully, son! They are only monkeys and not ghosts! So do not be frightened now. There are no ghosts. It is only an illusion."

After this incident, Balu became a brave boy and was never frightened of anything.

> **NEVER BELIEVE ANYTHING WITHOUT VERIFYING THE FACT**

STORIES FOR CHILDREN

All the stories in these books are selected from the 'Panchatantra', 'Hitopadesh', 'Aesop's Fables', 'Kathasaritsagar' and the traditional folk literature from all over the country and abroad. These stories are written in simple, lucid and attractive style so as to encourage self-reading in children. Besides, each story is adorned with lovely colourful illustrations.

These stories will gratify the curiosity and the tender feelings of children and also enrich their intellectual development.

A SET OF 5 BOOKS

A SET OF 5 BOOKS

A SET OF 5 BOOKS

A SET OF 7 BOOKS

A SET OF 5 BOOKS

A SET OF 5 BOOKS

STE 1

Printed by Maruti Printers, Ahmedabad. 12 1